CREATE
SHARE
INSPIRE

Notebook
Volume I, Issue 1

EDITORS: Ellyn Mansfield and Judi Weingarden

COVER AND INTERIOR DESIGN:
Kristin Omdahl

ILLUSTRATION: Kristin Omdahl

@ 2018 Kristin Omdahl
All rights reserved

Kristin Omdahl
18780 Trade Way Four
Ste 107-301
Bonita Springs, FL 34135
KristinOmdahl.com

Manufactured in USA

Library of Congress Cataloging-in-Publication Data
Omdahl, Kristin.
Create Share Inspire Notebook: Volume I, Issue 1 / Kristin Omdahl

Includes index
ISBN-13: 978-1721946587

ISBN-10: 1721946586

1. Diaries, Journals & Notebooks 2. Notebooks & Writing Pads

I feel so much more confident and in control of my life when I focus my awareness on the present moment, and assess my feelings calmly in conjunction with my gratitude and my goals. Recording and documenting your ideas is very important in the creative process. As you gain confidence you may find your creative thoughts bringing you closer to a happier life.

Journaling contributes to evoking mindfulness, healing, achieving goals, strengthening self-discipline, and improving memory and comprehension. Gratitude, when combined with journaling, greatly strengthens these benefits.

I believe human beings are more alike than they are different. During my lifelong quest for inspiration, I have discovered that throughout history there have been amazing people who agree with me.

I hope you enjoy the quotations I curated for this notebook. May they spark your inspiration as you begin to write each day. The theme for Volume I, Issue 1 is love. Unconditional love of self is the foundation from which all other love grows. Having faith in yourself is the key to unconditional love. Even if it has been a long time since you were kind to yourself, it only takes one moment, one thought, one act of kindness, to begin. So let's get started.

Let us make time to *create, share and inspire* today and every day.

Suggestions for How to Use Each Notebook

Two components of contentment are gratitude and being present in the moment. Daily practice helps in learning to be consistently mindful and focused. Hold your notebook closed, and take a few moments to allow your thoughts to settle and rest on your intentions for the day.

- Open the book to the day's page and read the inspirational quote.
- Write down your reactions to the quote: how it makes you feel; what it makes you think; or how you imagine it might influence your intentions.
- Jot down images or details about a creative project you are planning or would like to enhance.
- Make notes about something you would like to do for someone else.
- Write an affirmation of love to yourself.
- Or, write whatever motivates you or inspires you in some way.

Keep the notebook handy to jot down any other ideas you might have throughout the day. Remember that this is YOUR opportunity to *Create, Share and Inspire* in the ways you choose!

Each of the thirty-one days of this notebook has its own inspirational quote. The pages are not dated. Please start any time, any place, on any day that is right for you.

Each notebook has a *goals & intentions* section at the beginning and a *reflections* section at the end. Use these areas to focus on the bigger picture. If you are new to journaling the process may seem difficult or challenging at first, but rest assured that like anything else, it gets easier with practice. Keep all of your notebooks for future reference.

Kristin Omdahl is committed to helping fellow survivors of domestic violence and shedding light on this frightening, hidden crime in our society. In an attempt to achieve these goals and help eradicate domestic violence, Kristin will donate a portion of the proceeds from this book and all Kristin Omdahl products to the fund she established: **Project Kristin Cares.**

All funds collected by Project Kristin Cares will be donated to help survivors of domestic violence.

GOALS

INTENTIONS

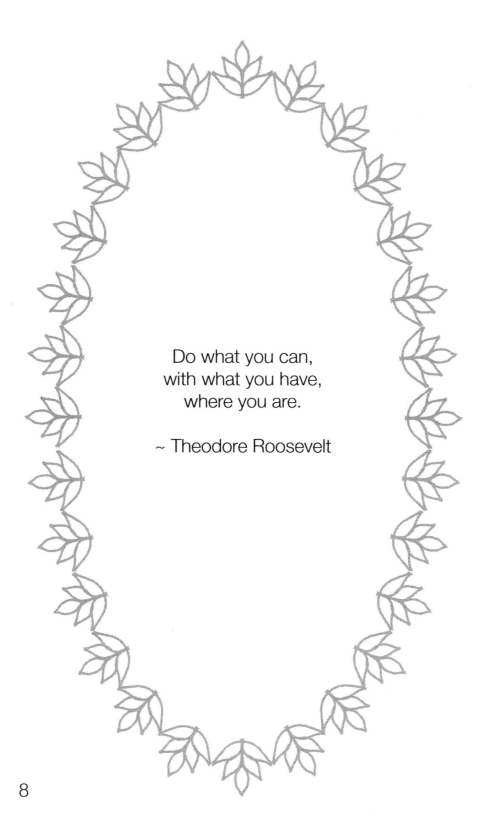

Do what you can,
with what you have,
where you are.

~ Theodore Roosevelt

| SUN | MON | TUES | WED | THURS | FRI | SAT |

Month   Day   Year

CREATE
SHARE
INSPIRE

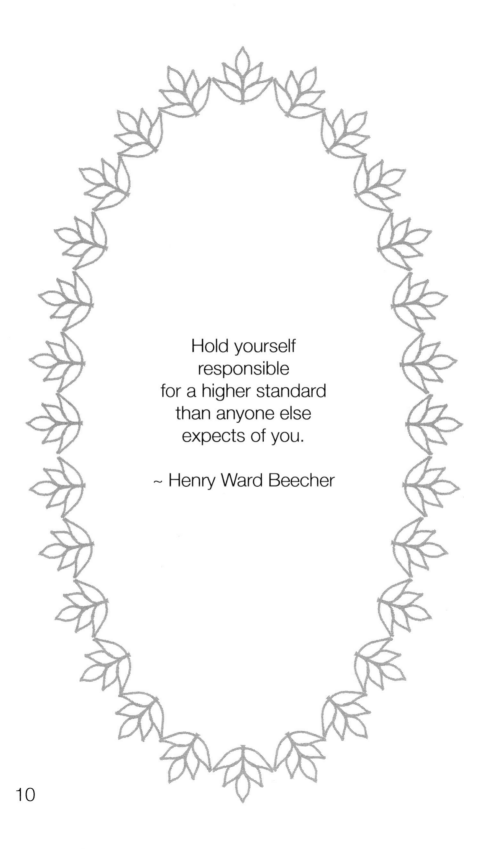

Hold yourself
responsible
for a higher standard
than anyone else
expects of you.

~ Henry Ward Beecher

SUN   MON   TUES   WED   THURS   FRI   SAT

Month   Day   Year

CREATE
SHARE
INSPIRE

Fall seven times.
Get up eight.

~ Japanese Proverb

| SUN | MON | TUES | WED | THURS | FRI | SAT |

Month Day Year

CREATE
SHARE
INSPIRE

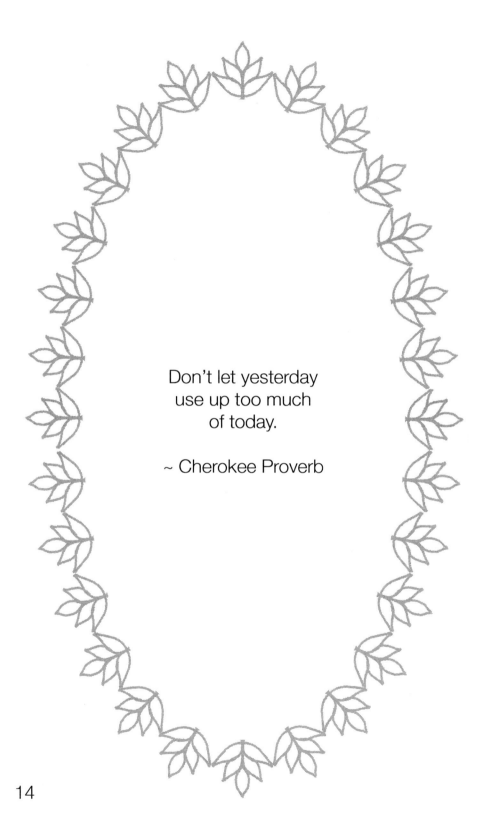

Don't let yesterday
use up too much
of today.

~ Cherokee Proverb

| SUN | MON | TUES | WED | THURS | FRI | SAT |

Month   Day   Year

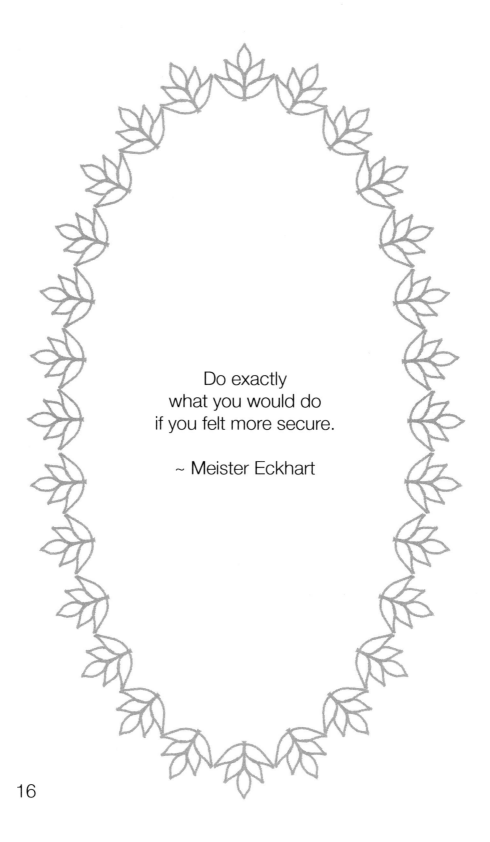

Do exactly
what you would do
if you felt more secure.

~ Meister Eckhart

| SUN | MON | TUES | WED | THURS | FRI | SAT |

Month   Day   Year

CREATE
SHARE
INSPIRE

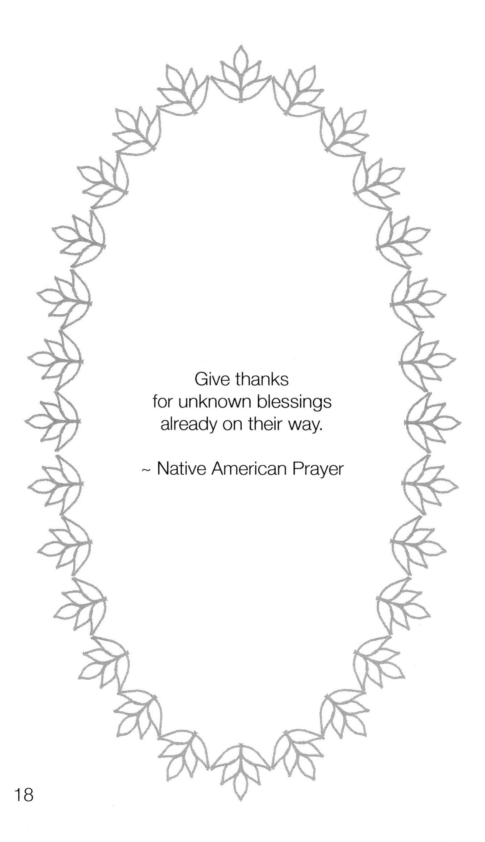

Give thanks
for unknown blessings
already on their way.

~ Native American Prayer

SUN   MON   TUES   WED   THURS   FRI   SAT

Month   Day   Year

CREATE
SHARE
INSPIRE

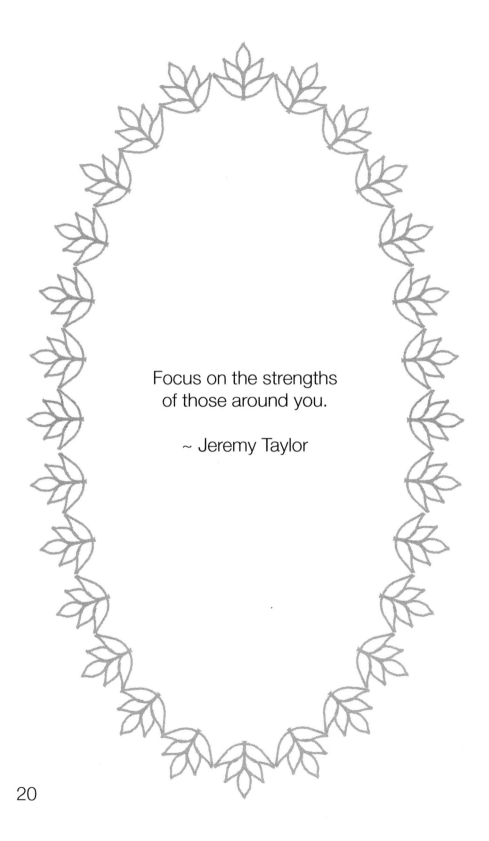

Focus on the strengths
of those around you.

~ Jeremy Taylor

| SUN | MON | TUES | WED | THURS | FRI | SAT |

Month   Day   Year

CREATE
SHARE
INSPIRE

Everybody
loves a compliment.

~ Abraham Lincoln

| SUN | MON | TUES | WED | THURS | FRI | SAT |

Month   Day   Year

CREATE
SHARE
INSPIRE

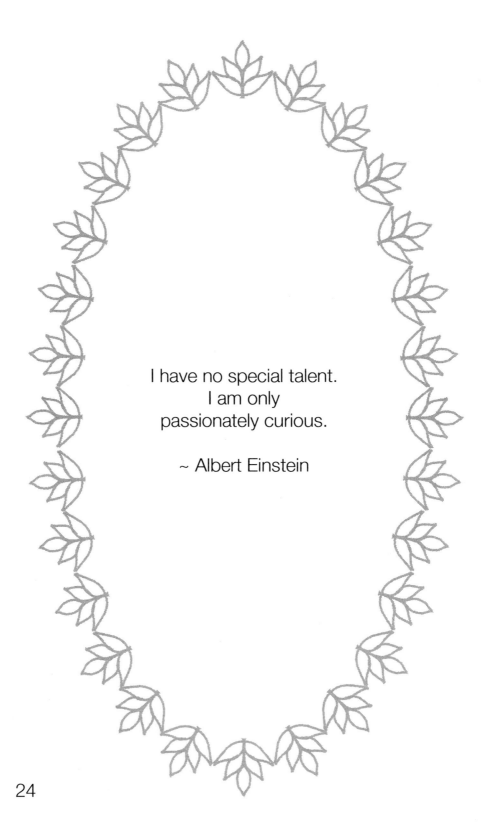

I have no special talent.
I am only
passionately curious.

~ Albert Einstein

SUN MON TUES WED THURS FRI SAT

Month   Day   Year

CREATE
SHARE
INSPIRE

Pleasure in the job
puts perfection
in the work.

~ Aristotle

| SUN | MON | TUES | WED | THURS | FRI | SAT |

Month   Day   Year

CREATE
SHARE
INSPIRE

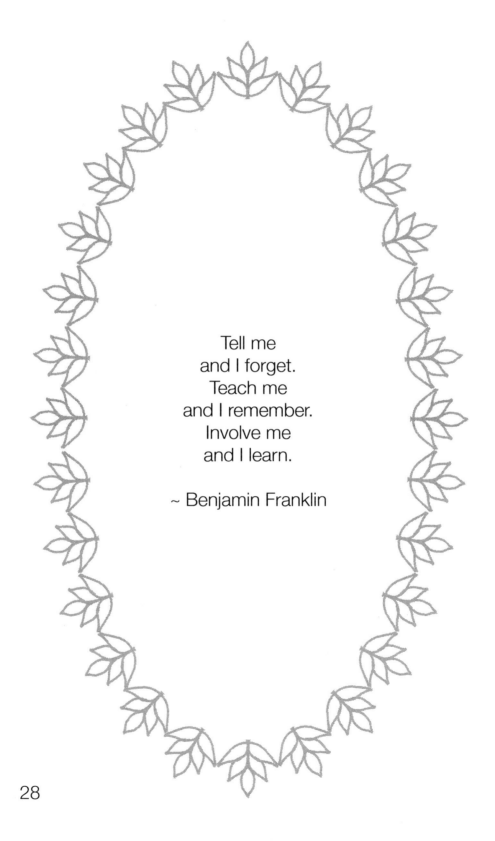

Tell me
and I forget.
Teach me
and I remember.
Involve me
and I learn.

~ Benjamin Franklin

| SUN | MON | TUES | WED | THURS | FRI | SAT |

Month   Day   Year

CREATE
SHARE
INSPIRE

Wherever you go,
go with all your heart.

~ Confucius

SUN   MON   TUES   WED   THURS   FRI   SAT

Month   Day   Year

CREATE
SHARE
INSPIRE

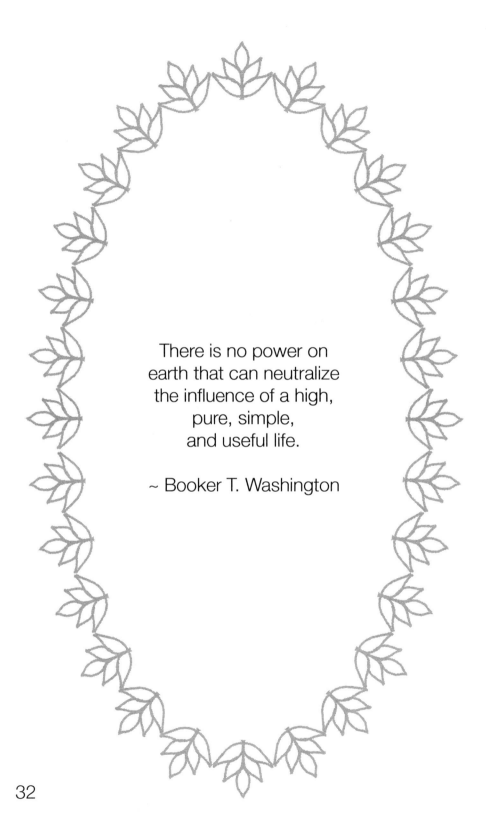

There is no power on
earth that can neutralize
the influence of a high,
pure, simple,
and useful life.

~ Booker T. Washington

| SUN | MON | TUES | WED | THURS | FRI | SAT |

Month   Day   Year

CREATE
SHARE
INSPIRE

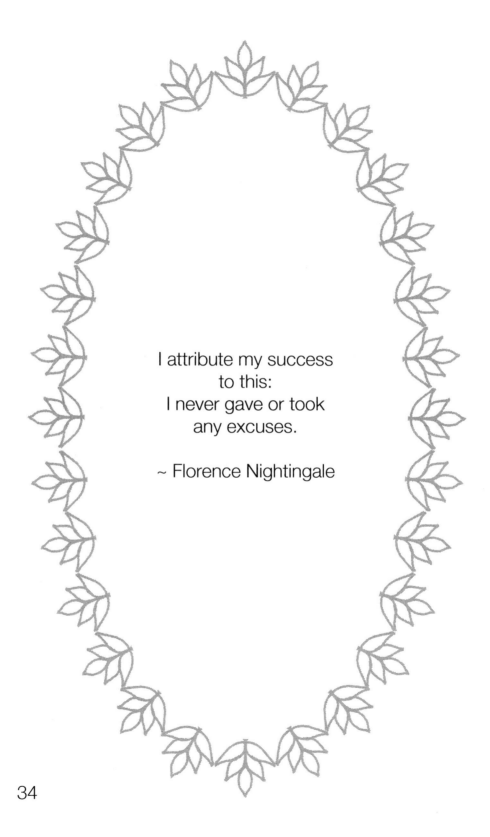

I attribute my success
to this:
I never gave or took
any excuses.

~ Florence Nightingale

| SUN | MON | TUES | WED | THURS | FRI | SAT |

Month   Day   Year

CREATE
SHARE
INSPIRE

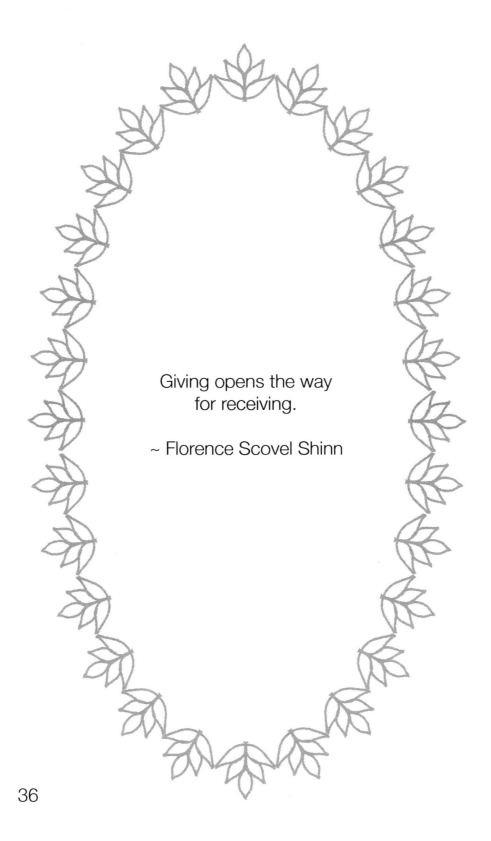

Giving opens the way
for receiving.

~ Florence Scovel Shinn

| SUN | MON | TUES | WED | THURS | FRI | SAT |

Month   Day   Year

CREATE
SHARE
INSPIRE

All the darkness
in the world
cannot extinguish the
light of a single candle.

~ Francis of Assisi

SUN   MON   TUES   WED   THURS   FRI   SAT

Month   Day   Year

CREATE
SHARE
INSPIRE

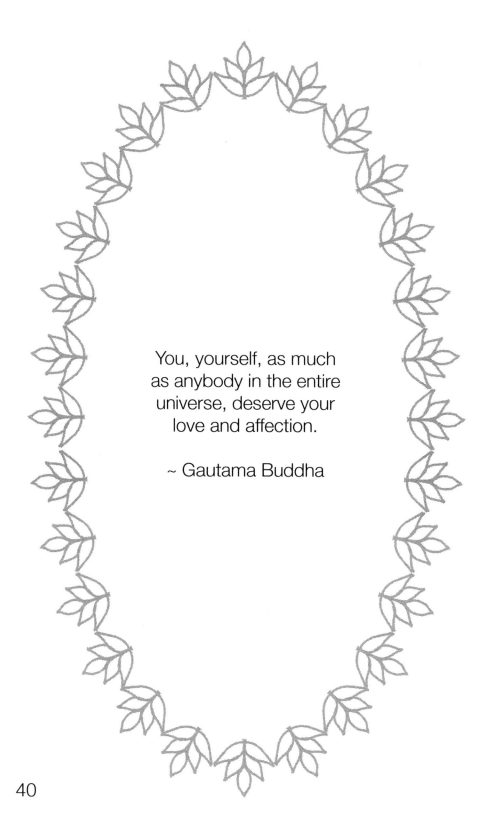

You, yourself, as much as anybody in the entire universe, deserve your love and affection.

~ Gautama Buddha

SUN   MON   TUES   WED   THURS   FRI   SAT

Month   Day   Year

CREATE
SHARE
INSPIRE

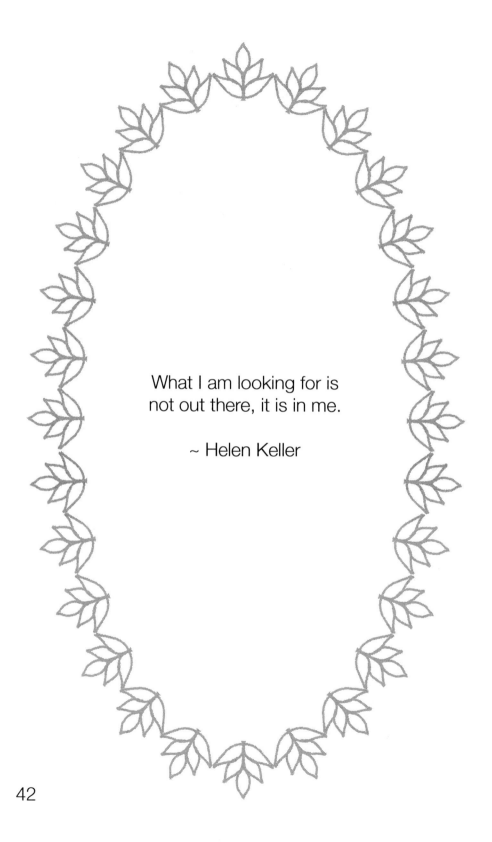

What I am looking for is
not out there, it is in me.

~ Helen Keller

SUN   MON   TUES   WED   THURS   FRI   SAT

Month   Day   Year

CREATE
SHARE
INSPIRE

Friendship is always
a sweet responsibility,
never an opportunity.

~ Khalil Gibran

| SUN | MON | TUES | WED | THURS | FRI | SAT |

Month Day Year

CREATE
SHARE
INSPIRE

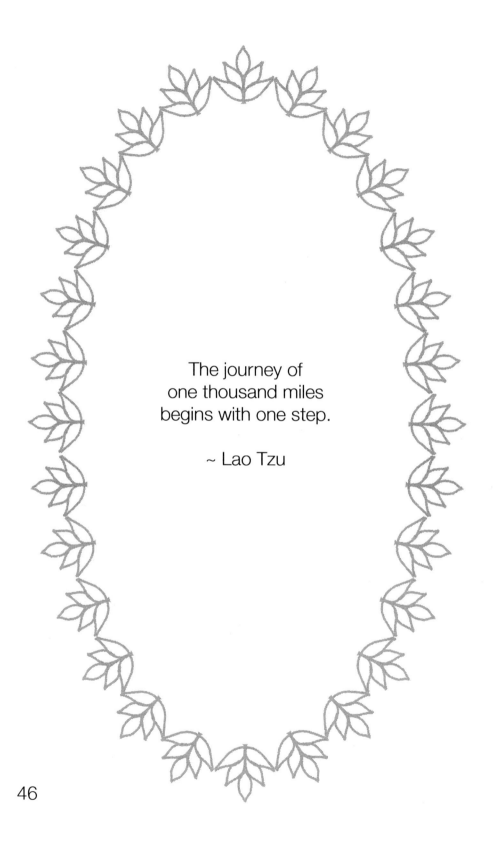

The journey of
one thousand miles
begins with one step.

~ Lao Tzu

SUN　MON　TUES　WED　THURS　FRI　SAT

Month　　　Day　　　Year

CREATE
SHARE
INSPIRE

The best way
to find yourself
is to lose yourself
in the service of others.

~ Mahatma Gandhi

| SUN | MON | TUES | WED | THURS | FRI | SAT |

Month   Day   Year

CREATE SHARE INSPIRE

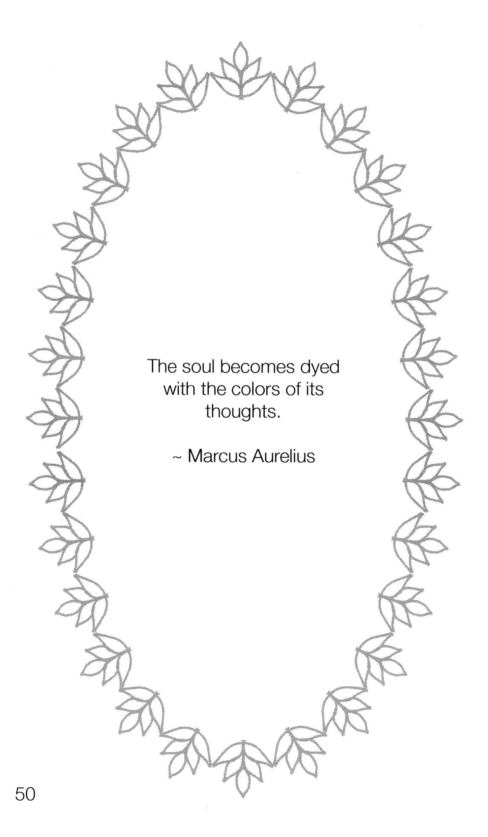

The soul becomes dyed with the colors of its thoughts.

~ Marcus Aurelius

SUN   MON   TUES   WED   THURS   FRI   SAT

Month   Day   Year

CREATE SHARE INSPIRE

Kindness is the language
which the dead can hear
and the blind can see.

~ Mark Twain

| SUN | MON | TUES | WED | THURS | FRI | SAT |

Month   Day   Year

CREATE
SHARE
INSPIRE

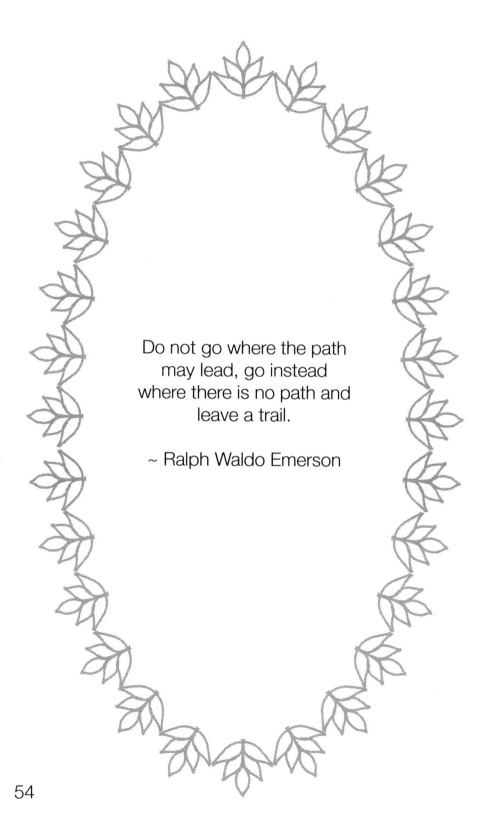

Do not go where the path may lead, go instead where there is no path and leave a trail.

~ Ralph Waldo Emerson

| SUN | MON | TUES | WED | THURS | FRI | SAT |

Month   Day   Year

CREATE
SHARE
INSPIRE

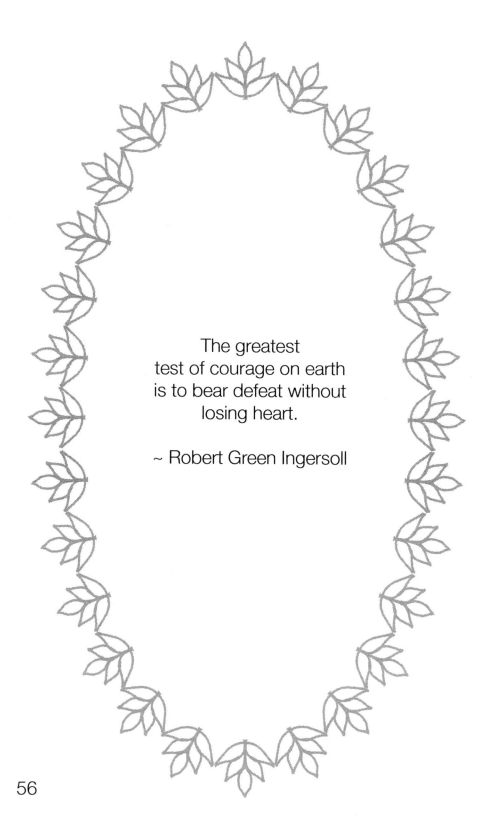

The greatest
test of courage on earth
is to bear defeat without
losing heart.

~ Robert Green Ingersoll

| SUN | MON | TUES | WED | THURS | FRI | SAT |

Month   Day   Year

CREATE
SHARE
INSPIRE

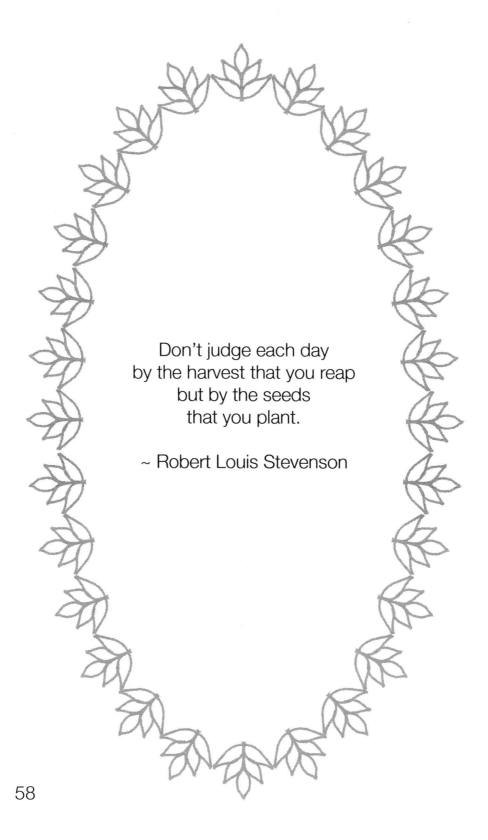

Don't judge each day
by the harvest that you reap
but by the seeds
that you plant.

~ Robert Louis Stevenson

| SUN | MON | TUES | WED | THURS | FRI | SAT |

Month　　　　　　Day　　　　　　　　Year

CREATE
SHARE
INSPIRE

Talk to yourself at least once a day. Otherwise you may miss a meeting with an excellent person in this world.

~ Swami Vivekananda

| SUN | MON | TUES | WED | THURS | FRI | SAT |

Month Day Year

CREATE SHARE INSPIRE

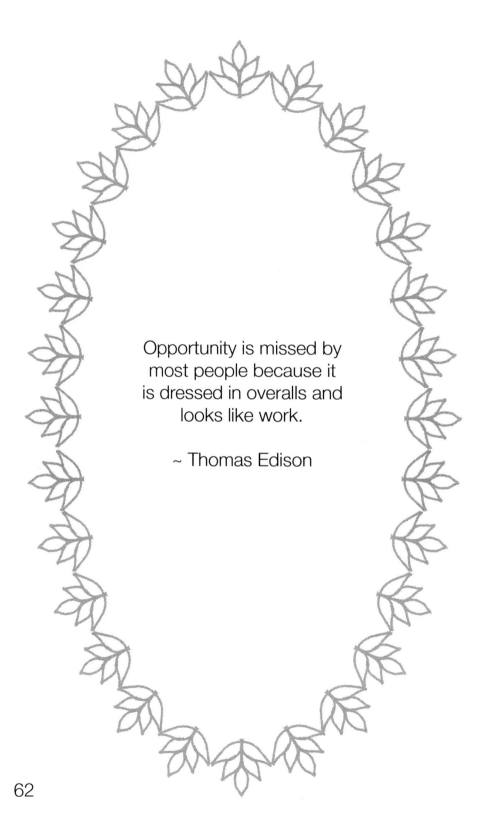

Opportunity is missed by most people because it is dressed in overalls and looks like work.

~ Thomas Edison

| SUN | MON | TUES | WED | THURS | FRI | SAT |

Month　　　　　Day　　　　　Year

CREATE
SHARE
INSPIRE

When angry, count to
ten before you speak.
If very angry,
count to one hundred.

~ Thomas Jefferson

| SUN | MON | TUES | WED | THURS | FRI | SAT |

Month　　　　　Day　　　　　　　Year

CREATE
SHARE
INSPIRE

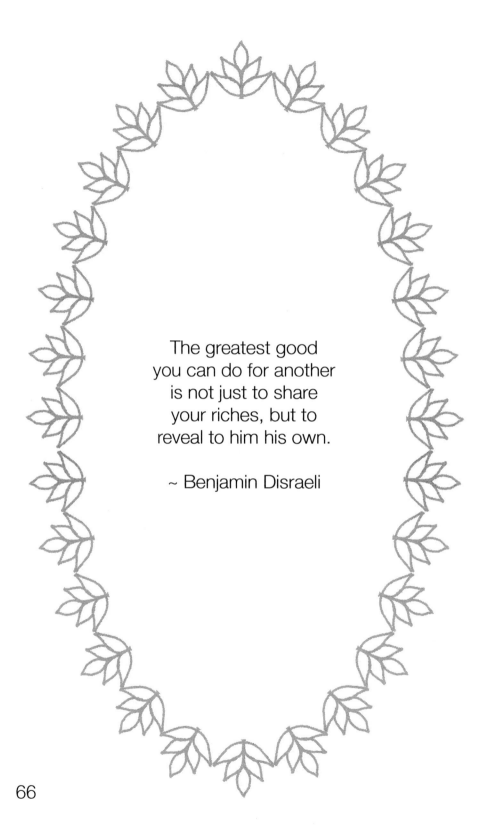

The greatest good
you can do for another
is not just to share
your riches, but to
reveal to him his own.

~ Benjamin Disraeli

| SUN | MON | TUES | WED | THURS | FRI | SAT |

Month   Day   Year

CREATE
SHARE
INSPIRE

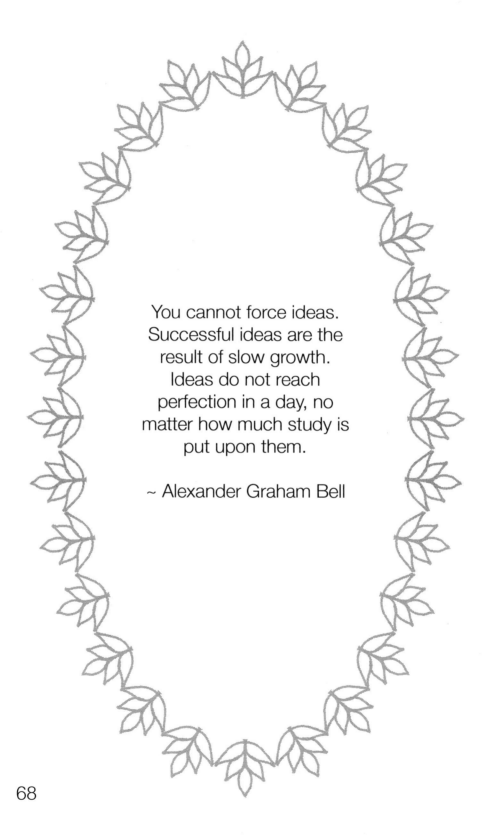

You cannot force ideas. Successful ideas are the result of slow growth. Ideas do not reach perfection in a day, no matter how much study is put upon them.

~ Alexander Graham Bell

SUN   MON   TUES   WED   THURS   FRI   SAT

Month   Day   Year

CREATE
SHARE
INSPIRE

REFLECTIONS

Index

Aristotle	26	Intentions	7
Aurelius, Marcus	50	Introduction	3
Beecher, Henry Ward	10	Japanese Proverb	12
Bell, Alexander Graham	68	Jefferson, Thomas	64
Buddha, Gautama	40	Keller, Helen	42
Cherokee Proverb	14	Lincoln, Abraham	22
Confucius	30	Native American Proverb	18
Disraeli, Benjamin	66	Nightingale, Florence	34
Eckhart, Meister	16	Project Kristin Cares	5
Edison, Thomas	62	Reflections	70, 71
Einstein, Albert	24	Roosevelt, Theodore	8
Emerson, Ralph Waldo	54	Scovel Shinn, Florence	36
Francis of Assisi	38	Stevenson, Robert Louis	58
Franklin, Benjamin	28	Suggested Uses	4
Gandhi, Mahatma	48	Taylor, Jeremy	20
Gibran, Khalil	44	Twain, Mark	52
Goals	6	Tzu, Lao	46
Ingersoll, Robert Green	56	Vivekananda, Swami	60
Introduction	3	Washington, Booker T.	32

Longing for more inspiration from Kristin?

Look no further.

@KristinOmdahl

Other titles by Kristin Omdahl:

Create Share Inspire, Volume I, Issues 1 - 5, 2018

Crea Comparte Inspira, Volumen I, Periódicas 1 - 5, 2018

Layers, Volume 1, 2018

Motif Magic, Volume 1, 2018

Continuous Crochet, 2016

Crochet So Lovely, 2015

Zen Art: A Coloring Book, 2015

I Taught Myself to Knit 18" Doll Clothes, 2015

I Taught Myself to Crochet 18" Doll Clothes, 2015

Beginners Guide to Knitting in the Round, 2014

Knitting Outside the Swatch, 2013

The Finer Edge, 2013

Complements Collection, 2012

A Knitting Wrapsody, 2011

Seamless Crochet, 2011

Crochet So Fine, 2010

Wrapped In Crochet, 2008

www.KristinOmdahl.com

Scan this QR code
for a special message
from Kristin

Made in the USA
Middletown, DE
03 August 2018